THE LIBRARY
ST. MARY'S COLLEGE OF MARYLAND
ST. MARY'S CITY, MARYLAND 20686

D1787783

THE VIEW FROM HERE

by

Margaret Dulaney

SAMUEL FRENCH, INC.
45 WEST 25TH STREET   NEW YORK 10010
7623 SUNSET BOULEVARD HOLLYWOOD 90046
LONDON   TORONTO

Copyright © 1990, 1993 by Margaret Dulaney Balitsaris

ALL RIGHTS RESERVED

CAUTION: Professionals and amateurs are hereby warned that THE VIEW FROM HERE is subject to a royalty. It is fully protected under the copyright laws of the United States of America, the British Commonwealth, including Canada, and all other countries of the Copyright Union. All rights, including professional, amateur, motion picture, recitation, lecturing, public reading, radio broadcasting, television, and the rights of translation into foreign languages are strictly reserved. In its present form the play is dedicated to the reading public only.

The amateur live stage performance rights to THE VIEW FROM HERE are controlled exclusively by Samuel French, Inc., and royalty arrangements and licenses must be secured well in advance of presentation. PLEASE NOTE that amateur royalty fees are set upon application in accordance with your producing circumstances. When applying for a royalty quotation and license please give us the number of performances intended, dates of production, your seating capacity and admission fee. Royalties are payable one week before the opening performance of the play to Samuel French, Inc., at 45 W. 25th Street, New York, NY 10010-2751; or at 7623 Sunset Blvd., Hollywood, CA 90046-2795, or to Samuel French (Canada), Ltd., 80 Richmond Street East, Toronto, Ontario, Canada M5C 1P1.

Royalty of the required amount must be paid whether the play is presented for charity or gain and whether or not admission is charged.

Stock royalty quoted on application to Samuel French, Inc.

For all other rights than those stipulated above, apply to Bret Adams Ltd., 448 W. 44th St., New York, NY 10036.

Particular emphasis is laid on the question of amateur or professional readings, permission and terms for which must be secured in writing from Samuel French, Inc.

Copying from this book in whole or in part is strictly forbidden by law, and the right of performance is not transferable.

Whenever the play is produced the following notice must appear on all programs, printing and advertising for the play: "Produced by special arrangement with Samuel French, Inc."

Due authorship credit must be given on all programs, printing and advertising for the play.

ISBN 0 573 69447-8   Printed in U.S.A.

Dedicated to:
My husband Matt
for his tenacious understanding.

No one shall commit or authorize any act or omission by which the copyright of, or the right to copyright, this play may be impaired.
No one shall make any changes in this play for the purpose of production.
Publication of this play does not imply availability for performance. Both amateurs and professionals considering a production are *strongly* advised in their own interests to apply to Samuel French, Inc., for written permission before starting rehearsals, advertising, or booking a theatre.
No part of this book may be reproduced, stored in a retrieval system, or transmitted in any form, by any means, now known or yet to be invented, including mechanical, electronic, photocopying, recording, videotaping, or otherwise, without the prior written permission of the publisher.

IMPORTANT BILLING AND CREDIT REQUIREMENTS

All producers of THE VIEW FROM HERE *must* give credit to the Author of the Play in all programs distributed in connection with performances of the Play and in all instances in which the title of the Play appears for purposes of advertising, publicizing or otherwise exploiting the Play and/or a production. The name of the Author *must* also appear on a separate line, on which no other name appears, immediately following the title, and *must* appear in size of type not less than fifty percent the size of the title type.

The following credit must appear in all programs:

"The View From Here" was originally produced by the Lamb's Theatre Company, Carolyn Rossi-Copeland, Producing Artistic Director, in association with Novi Productions, Inc."

The View From Here received a workshop at Actor's Theatre of Louisville in June 1990 with the following cast:

FERN .... Mary Catherine Wright
MAPLE .... Peggity Price
CARLA .... Adale O'Brien
ARNOLD .... William McNulty

Director: Betsy Schevey
Dramaturg: Michael Dixon
Stage Manager: Frazier Marsh

The View From Here was presented by The University of Evansville Theatre, October 2-11, 1992 with the following cast:

FERN .... Karla D. Williams
MAPLE .... Leigh Green
CARLA .... Sheryl Anderson
ARNOLD .... Patrick Kelly

Directed by John David Lutz
Scenery designed by Joseph P. Flauto
Costumes designed by Patti McCrory
Lighting designed by Tabitha Rodman
Sound designed by C. Farlow Perry
Original Music by Matt Balitsaris
Stage Manager: Printha K. McCallum

The View From Here was produced by Lamb's Theatre Company, New York City, Caroline Rossi Copeland, Producing Artistic Director, in association with Novi Productions, Inc. Opening night was February 25, 1993 with the following cast:

FERN .... Angelina Fiordellisi
MAPLE .... Lily Knight
CARLA .... Tudi Roche
ARNOLD .... Adam Lefevre

Directed by Matt Williams
Scenery designed by Michael Anania
Costumes designed by Elsa Ward
Lighting designed by Michael Gilliam
Original Music by Matt Balitsaris
Sound designed by Tristan Wilson
Production Stage Manager: Karen Moore

CHARACTERS

FERN — woman in her thirties, who has been an agoraphobic for six years.

MAPLE — Fern's baby sister, who has been in a catatonic state for two days.

CARLA — Fern's up the street neighbor, in her late thirties.

ARNOLD — Fern's across the street neighbor, in his late thirties/early forties.

ACT I
Fern's livingroom

Sc. 1: Early morning
Sc. 2: Later that day
Sc. 3: That evening

ACT II
The same

Sc. 1: Later the same night
Sc. 2: The following morning
Sc. 3: Four weeks later, evening

SET DESIGN

The play takes place in the mid Eighties in a small town in Kentucky. There is one set. It is Fern's living room. The most important set pieces are the front door, which should have a screen door that is always used, with the main door propped open. A couch which could conceivably sleep a grown man. A television, facing upstage. A telephone with a long stretchy cord from receiver to base. And tons of baby paraphernalia, two or three cribs, a playpen, stuffed animals, wind-up mobiles, disposable diaper boxes, etc. Besides the screen door there are two other entrances. One leads to the bedroom and bathroom, and the other to the kitchen. These two entrances could be combined to lead to all three offstage locations.

THE VIEW FROM HERE

ACT I

Scene 1

It is a hot summer morning. Hot and humid.

A small LIGHT comes up on FERN, who is looking through binoculars out the screen door. MAPLE sits in a catatonic state on the couch. Throughout much of this first scene FERN'S physical behavior should be restless, like that of a caged animal. After a while, FERN puts the binoculars down and speaks to the audience.

FERN. It was just after my 28th birthday that I began my life as a fruitcake ... I was out at the Kroger's on Dixie Highway, when it all started. I'd gone in for a can of tuna and a *Glamour* magazine. Now, I'd noticed I'd been feeling a little funny in grocery stores lately, kinda crossed-eyed, you know, but this time it was as if ... as if—WHAM!—the earth dive-bombed into another part of space and my shoes weren't sticky enough to hold me on. Tried to get a grip on myself. Figured maybe I just needed to focus on what I'd come in for, see. So, I find the *Glamour* pretty easy, and head out through the fluorescent nightmare towards the canned goods, trying to suck my eyeballs back into my head so I could see better. Finally I make it, look over to where the tuna should be, and it seems they've reorganized their shelves, and I'm staring with horror at a box of Co-Co Puffs. Well, that's when all hell breaks loose in my head. The linoleum starts swimming around under my feet. The aisles begin to cave in. Fruit Loops are closing in on me. I head for the exit—Muzak throbbing—grocery carts forming blockades—I pick up my pace—dodging housewives—tripping over children—I see a giant toilet paper pyramid in front of me—I hurdle it—stomp on the rubber stuff—and I'm free ... Next thing I know, I'm leaning on the inside of that door there ... Yeah ... It was as quiet as a coffin in here that day. (*Pause.*) After a while, I noticed the *Glamour* magazine all scrambled up in my hands. Now, I have never, ever, ever, stolen one blessed thing in all my life. Mama used to say, "If you wanna know what it's like going through life without a rear-end, just try stealing something." There are two things that I have never in my life done, and those are, one, steal, and two, eat a booger. So you see, if my behavior in the Kroger's was not enough to convince me that I'd gone mental, the fact that I had run out without paying for that magazine left no room for doubt. I, at the age of twenty-eight, out at the Kroger's on Dixie Highway, had slipped into La-La Land. (*SHE glances out the screen door, as the LIGHTS begin to come up on the rest of the room.)* Lord, will you look at that? That must be their whole bedroom suit marching out the door.

(The LIGHTS have come up to full morning light. MAPLE sits on the couch staring at the T.V. with a remote control in her lap. The T.V. should be barely audible, but we should be able to make out that SHE is watching cartoons, preferably the Jetsons.)

FERN. Good night, what's he gonna sleep on? The couch walked out five minutes ago ... 'Course, who'd wanna sleep on that old plastic thing, anyway? You'd stick to it, for one. Wake up freezing with the couch wearing a couple of layers of your skin. *(Out the door.)* Don't imagine he'll miss that Tupperware furniture! *(FERN hits the floor and crawls away from the door. The LIGHTS go down on the room, and the sound of the T.V. fades, as a LIGHT comes back up on FERN, SHE speaks to the audience.)* It was some time, you can imagine, before I could focus on the cover story of my mutilated *Glamour* magazine, but there it was, just as clear a sign from the man upstairs as you'd ever wanna look for. "AGORAPHOBIA, FEAR OF THE MARKET PLACE. DOT DOT DOT, A CRIPPLING AFFLICTION." That's A-G-O-R-A-phobia. Mama says it always sounds to her like I have a fear of farming. So, I open it up and read how there are people all across the country who are holed up in their houses 'cause of this fear, see, this agoraphobia business. We're talking perfectly intelligent people, who when faced with going out and picking up a couple of things for dinner, would sooner fry up their house pets ... Well, I'm thinking this over, when the phone rings and it's Mama on the other end saying, "Hello, Fern, honey, what's crackin'?" So I say, "Me, Mama, I'm crackin'!" and I start to tell her all about the linoleum and the Co-Co Puffs, and the cart blockades, when she stops me and says, "Don't worry, honey, I was just this minute headed out to the Winn Dixie on Central Parkway. What was it you needed?" (*SHE shrugs her shoulders as the LIGHTS begin to come back up to full morning.*) Welp, that was six years ago, and I'm still stuck in here watching the world scoot past my front door ... I always did love a view.

(*FERN moves to the door and raises her binoculars to her face. The LIGHTS have come up to full and FERN no longer addresses the audience. MAPLE has not moved a muscle.*)

FERN. Oh my God, what's this? Maple you've gotta come look at this! It's one of those butt jiggler things, like Mama used to have! Remember? It had a belt type thing you wrapped around your backside, and it was s'posed to jiggle away your poundage. (*SHE demonstrates.*) We used to use it on our heads, remember? (*Out the screen door.*) Give up darlin'! Nothing short of the atom bomb gonna put a dent in that thing! (*FERN hits the floor again, and crawls over to the couch.*) Don't worry, Maple, she can't hear me.

(*No response from MAPLE.*)

FERN. She's moving out on her husband, Arnold Palmer. They just moved in a couple of months back. His name's not really Arnold Palmer, we just call him that, 'cause he's always either going or coming back from the links. You can tell, cause he wears those cleaty shoes, and sports a whole closet-load of some of the most Godawful clothes you'd ever wanna see.

(*The PHONE rings and MAPLE looks blankly at Fern.*)

FERN. Hold that thought. (*SHE moves away and picks up the phone. A plate of cookies sits by the phone.*) Fern's Fun House, how may I help you? ... Oh, hello Mama ... Oh yeah, she's up, and may I say she is the picture of animation this morning ... Uh huh ... Yeah, well I tried that ... (*FERN picks up one of the cookies and hurls it at Maple.*) Think fast!

(*MAPLE ducks.*)

FERN. She's alive! Thank you Jesus! (*Back to phone.*) .... Huh? ... Well it's nap time at the present ... (*FERN walks over and looks in one of the cribs.*) Oh, I've been wallowing in domestic drudgery this morning. You know if you leave something in the back of the fridge long enough it grows hair? (*FERN chuckles. To Maple.*) Mama says you might want to let your husband in on that secret, Maple. (*Watching Maple. Back to phone.*) You know, if this child went any slower she'd be going backwards ... Uh huh ... tried that too, yeah ... (*SHE looks back out the screen door.*) Get a load of that! (*SHE drops the phone and runs to the door for a better look.*) She's taking the microwave! My God, that's low. The microwave.

(*Pause. The PHONE starts screaming. FERN runs to pick it up.*)

FERN. You remember to enter me in that microwave raffle out at the Super Kroger's? ... You're a doll. You enter yourself? ... Well I hope I win, you lose ... What? On the T.V.? ... What time they picking it? ... Uh huh ... Oh, here comes Carla from up the street, I'd better jump. Later. (*SHE hangs up.*) Maple, honey, try and look a little more lively for company, would you? Carla has never encountered a dead person on my couch before. (*FERN fluffs Maple like a pillow.*)

(*CARLA pokes her head in the door.*)

CARLA. Paper girl. (*SHE waves Fern's newspaper in the air.*) I was headed over to the 7-Eleven, wondered did you need anything. Ooops. (*Covers her mouth and whispers.*) Is it nap-nap time?

FERN. Don't worry, Carla, you couldn't wake the Brainard twins with a family tragedy. Watch this. (*FERN leans over the cribs and screams.*) Wake up, boys! Your Mama just blew up! Little pieces of her all over the front yard! ... See?

CARLA. I wonder does Ellen Brainard know you do that. (*Moves into the room and sees Maple.*) Oh, 'scuse me, didn't know you had company. Hi there, I'm Carla from up the street, and who might you be?

(*MAPLE stares at Carla with a kind of horror.*)

FERN. This is my baby sister, Maple.

CARLA. Well, hello, stranger!

FERN. Maple, this is Carla from up the street.

CARLA. I sure am happy to meet you, heard so much about you.

FERN. She's feeling kinda puny this morning 'cause her husband walked out on her.

CARLA. Oh, you poor thing.

FERN. Drove over from Versailles last night, and has been in a state of catatonia ever since. Maple, honey, try not to stare at our company, she's not on the T.V. ... Carla, I believe the hand of God delivered you over here this morning, I believe that entirely. Maple, this woman here's been walked out on more than the gangplank.

CARLA. It's true, sweetheart. I try and keep my spirits up though. Read somewhere, where this woman was so bent outa shape over this fellow walking out on her, she went—tracked him down—found his car parked outside the other woman's house, see—car was parked on a hill—pulled the emergency brake—ran around—laid herself in front—and let that car just roll right over her. (*Slight pause.*) To illustrate, see, exactly what she felt he'd done to her. Yep, you gotta keep your spirits up ... What'd he leave you for sweetie, another woman?

(MAPLE looks at Carla, gets up and moves over to where the cookies are. Grabs a huge knife as the other TWO gasp. Lays a cookie down and karate chops it in half. MAPLE puts half of the cookie she chopped in her mouth and mumbles with her mouth full.)

MAPLE. Monopoly.
CARLA. What's that?
FERN. Monogamy?
CARLA. Well, that's your number one killer, all right. Uh huh. There are very few fellows that will put up with that system.
MAPLE. Monopoly.
FERN. I believe she said Monopoly.
CARLA. Monopoly?
FERN. Did you say Monopoly, Maple?

(MAPLE slips back into her thoughts, and moves back to her spot on the couch.)

FERN. I'm not sure but what that's all we're gonna get out of her for the present.

(Pause, while FERN and CARLA study her.)

FERN. She's married to an astronomer.
CARLA. Is that right? ... Your husband's not that fellow writes for the *Versailles Voice*, is he?! Lord, I don't go out my door in the morning before I've read my horoscope in the *Versailles Voice*.

(MAPLE looks at her, blankly.)

FERN. I believe you're thinking of an astrologer, Carla. He's an astronomer. Stargazer.
CARLA. Oh, Uh huh ...
FERN. Truth is, he works at the produce section at the Piggly Wiggly during the day, but at night, he's out in their backyard with his face jammed in a telescope.
CARLA. Is that right?
FERN. Yeah, real interesting fellow.

(Pause as THEY both stare at Maple.)

FERN. *(Looks at the T.V.)* Maple, you're not gonna watch "Lost In Space," are you? Tell me you're not. Good night ... Poor thing's lost all sense and I'm trapped here in rerun hell.

(The PHONE rings and MAPLE reacts very slightly. FERN pats Maple on the shoulder.)

FERN. I'll get that. (*SHE answers the phone.*) Fern's Baby Coop, how may I help you? ... Yes, ma'am, I certainly do, as long as they're horizontal. How old is he? ... I'm sorry, ma'am, but once they get that age, they do crazy things like walk out front doors and that is beyond my ... my expertise, you might say. I sure am sorry ... Well, let me know if you drop another one. (*SHE hangs up and looks out the screen door.*) She must be winding down over there, there goes the weedeater.

CARLA. You notice she took the microwave?

FERN. Yes, bless his heart ... You know, he wouldn't be half bad, if he'd do something about that wardrobe of his—let his hair grow out a little—trade in that car—work on his posture ... What do you think he did?

CARLA. Played too much golf, I guess. Read in the paper, that golf is the upset of 10% of the failed marriages in the State of Kentucky. (*CARLA looks at Maple.*) Your husband play golf, Maple?

(MAPLE makes no response.)

CARLA. She clam up like this often?

FERN. Used to all the time, when she was little. Depending on how big a wound it was, she could go for days.
CARLA. Is that right?
FERN. Maple, Maple, "Lost In Space" ...? (*Pause as FERN gets drawn into the T.V.*)
CARLA. So what's gonna happen?
FERN. I believe this is the one where the robot gets de-programmed ...
CARLA. No, I mean with Maple?
FERN. Oh, she'll blow. She'll bust wide open. Could happen any minute.
CARLA. That right?
FERN. Yeah, it'll all come spilling out. Poor thing's been tossing it around in that head of her's like salad for so long, should be pretty messy.

(*THEY watch Maple for a moment.*)

FERN. Could happen any minute.

(*THEY watch her a little longer.
PHONE rings and again. MAPLE reacts slightly.*)

FERN. Good nightamighty. (*FERN picks up the phone.*) Fern's Five and Dime, how may I help you? ... Sir, there's no one lives here by the name Bernice ...

(*MAPLE grabs Carla's arm and shoots her a haunted look, which Fern does not see.*)

FERN. Can I ask what number you're trying to call? ... (*FERN snaps the handset of the phone away from her ear and looks at it.*) Weirdo! ... (*SHE slams the receiver down.*)

(*MAPLE relaxes her grip on Carla and stares back at the T.V. CARLA watches Maple carefully.*)

CARLA. World's lousy with 'em, Fern, I tell you what. (*Pause.*) Remember that fellow, packed up and moved out a couple of years ago, claimed he couldn't stand my table manners?
FERN. One with the hair?
CARLA. That's the one. (*Trying to include Maple.*) Kids in the neighborhood would bust out crying just to look at him. Scary hair ...

(*MAPLE stares at Carla for a moment, with a sort of horrified wonder.*)

CARLA. Scary hair ... Anyway, I was watching the local news last night. That woman with the lip liner on 15, you know the one. She was saying how this fellow was wanted for murdering his wife, see, and they finally tracked him down. Seems he killed her because, and I quote, "Could not stomach the manner in which she carried food to her mouth." (*Pause.*) Didn't hardly sleep a wink last night.
FERN. Was it your fellow with the scary hair?

CARLA. No, honey, my Lord no. It wasn't him.
FERN. Well, then why in the ...
CARLA. I just shudder to think how nearly I escaped death, just by pushing a little dinner around with my fingers ... Lord, don't get me started. (*CARLA looks out the door.*) Where do you suppose Arnold Palmer is through this whole thing?
FERN. I'd say he's probably tossing one down at the nineteenth hole right about now ... Gosh, I'd never get on my husband for playing golf. I believe I'd encourage an activity like that.
CARLA. You know, Fern, honey, you are going to make some man very happy one day. There's a man out there wandering around with the letters F.E.R.N. branded on his heart, and he's gonna recognize you, just the minute he lays eyes on you.
FERN. Well, I guess he's gonna have to wander around a little while longer, till I can get out to meet him.
CARLA. It's a wonder you never went to see someone about that ... that ... whatever the heck it is you call that what you have.
FERN. Oh, I don't trust those people, Carla. Daddy went to some fellow down on Sycamore cause he wasn't getting along with Mama. This fellow tells Daddy how he has to find out who *he* is, and how *he* can get *his* needs met, and let me tell you, within six months he was meeting just about every need that popped into his head, finally discovering his great primal need for Sandra

Winfries that worked out at the Dairy Queen on Chestnut. No, thank you, no, I believe I'll pass.

CARLA. Well, suit yourself, but it sure is a shame, only people get to benefit from you are a handful of ladies that bring the groceries by.

FERN. Good Lord, Carla, we already got one victim of paralyzing depression in here.

(THEY BOTH look at Maple.
MAPLE slumps over with her head in her lap.
THEY rush over to comfort her. Sitting on either side of her.)

FERN. Oh, Maple, honey ... You know they can't make it off that planet.

CARLA. Yeah, sweetheart, the series would be over.

FERN. I don't think they'd hold our interest if they went back to Cleveland, or wherever it is they're from, and just took up their lives again.

CARLA. Just think about the title, honey, "Lost in Space" ... Seems to me they're kinda committed to that, that, that ... concept, I guess you'd call it.

FERN. They'd have to call it, "Found in Cleveland."

CARLA. And who would give a dern, really?

FERN. Not a soul. The robot would have to go, for one ...

CARLA. Yeah, a robot would seem kinda out of place in Cleveland.

MAPLE. (*Stands up and lets out a high piercing scream.*) AAAAAAIIIIII!

(*The other TWO are frozen on the couch.*)

MAPLE. Told him I wasn't coming out of that bathroom till he could settle down. Hotels, houses, dice, flying around like bullets. Screaming: (*Imitates Stan's voice.*) "Re-match! Re-match!" Veins sticking up all over top of his head. "I want a re-match!" Launching little playing pieces out the door. (*SHE runs to the screen door and launches imaginary pieces one by one as SHE says.*) "I-WANT-A-GOD-DAMNED-RE-MATCH!!!" Pastel money's flying everywhere. Pink! Blue! Yellow! (*SHE runs back to the couch to explain to FERN and CARLA, who are stuck there, too overwhelmed to react.*) Heck, I couldn't help it I had a hotel on Marvin Gardens just seemed to suck him in every time he came around the board! He takes the board. (*MAPLE picks up a magazine.*) Spits on it. (*SHE spits on it.*) Curses at it. (*In Stan's voice.*) "Goddamned board!" Stomps on it. (*SHE lays the magazine down and jumps up and down on it.*) Rips it in half. (*Picks up the magazine and rips it in half.*) I ran—locked myself in the bathroom—Heard him kick everything in the room—finally kicks the front door open and slams out the door. Screams: (*In Stan's voice.*) "I'm disappointed in you, Maple! Just Goddamned disappointed!" (*MAPLE stands in the middle of the room panting. Suddenly SHE rushes over to the front door and yells out of it, loud enough so Stan can hear her in Versailles.)* So, I come home to Fern ... Stan, you stubborn ... buh ... you stupid stubborn ... buh ... you stupid stubborn stinky ... BUTTHEAD!!! *(SHE stands at the door for a moment and catches her breath. In a controlled voice.)* I think I'm gonna be sick. *(SHE runs in the bathroom.)*

(Pause.)

    FERN. I forgot about that part.
    CARLA. What part?
    FERN. The part where she has to go upchuck.
    CARLA. Damn.

(LIGHTS fade. End of Scene 1.)

ACT I

Scene 2

LIGHTS come up on FERN and MAPLE. FERN is following along with an aerobics program on the T.V., and MAPLE watches her. MAPLE still looks a little rough and seems preoccupied. It is later on that same day.

    FERN. Maple, why don't you get on up here with me? Do you some good.

MAPLE. My mouth may be working, but my body feels like hell.

FERN. Suit yourself. (*To the T.V.*) Shake that thing, Louise!!!

MAPLE. I worry about you all cooped up in here by yourself, Fern. Doesn't seem like much of a life for you.

FERN. (*Stops exercising for a moment.*) And who are you? The Life police?

MAPLE. You know what I ...

FERN. Sergeant You-Gotta-Be-In-It-To-Win-It?

MAPLE. You know what I mean, Fern.

FERN. (*Starts exercising again.*) Yeah, I know. Don't you waste your time worrying about me. Life's a gas.

MAPLE. Why the dickens you never went to see someone about that, I'll never ...

FERN. (*Stops exercising.*) Well how would I get there, Maple?! (*SHE turns off the T.V.*) Besides, the way I figure it, when the Man Upstairs feels it's time for me to go back out and join the world, he'll send me a clear sign, and I'll go. I believe that entirely.

MAPLE. Um hm ... You must be pretty lonesome for a man by now?

FERN. Well, sure. But I figure I'm no more lonesome than the girls out there dating every Tom, Dick, and Asshole, comes along.

MAPLE. Boy, I guess we both got a lot to look forward to.

FERN. Now, Maple, don't say that! You and Stan'll get back together. Hell, he's probably home right now, tearing his hair out, worried sick about you.
MAPLE. What hair?
FERN. Come on, Maple, why don't you try calling him? Go ahead. I'll go back in the bathroom and hum to myself, won't hear a word...

(The PHONE rings, and again MAPLE reacts slightly.)

FERN. This is probably him right now. (*Picks up phone.*) Fern's Fine Wearables, how may I help you? ... Sir, to the best of my knowledge, in the past six years, not one single person with the name Bernice has stepped across this threshold. Now, I have given this some careful thought since the last time you called, and I believe I can stand firmly behind that statement. Not one Bernice in six years. May I ask what Bernice's last name is? ... (*SHE holds the handset at arm's distance.*) Pervert!!! (*SHE slams down the receiver.*)

(Pause.)

MAPLE. Ever heard of Bernice's Hair?
FERN. That that beauty parlor out on Walnut? Carla went to that place, came back looking like a snow cone.
MAPLE. No, no, I'm talking about a bunch of stars, a constellation called Bernice's Hair.

FERN. Up in the sky?

MAPLE. Yeah, bunch of stars, supposed to look like hair. It's called Bernice's Hair.

FERN. Well, isn't that something. Stan tell you about that?

MAPLE. Uh, huh.

FERN. Bernice's Hair, huh ... Is it straight or kinky?

MAPLE. What?!

FERN. Her hair.

MAPLE. (*Snaps.*) I don't know, Fern, it's kinda hard to tell!

FERN. Well, Pardon-eh-moi!

CARLA. (*Pokes her head in the door.*) Aloha.

FERN. You missed aerobics.

CARLA. Well, pooh. (*CARLA moves into the room.*)

FERN. What you been doing?

CARLA. Been home tuned into my police scanner. Got a sick feeling something tragic's gonna happen today.

FERN. Why's that?

CARLA. It's the new moon. Read somewhere that the new moon messes up your sense of timing. It's like being in a time warp, see. You could think you were doing 55 when in actuality you're doing 155. Or, maybe someone's signalling for a turn, front of you, and you're thinking you got plenty of time to slow down, but that's just exactly where you're messed up, see, and there's a ten to one chance you'd mow that poor son-of-a-bitch down all on account of it's being your new moon ... Yep ... I haven't been in a car on the day of the new moon in over three years.

MAPLE. Three years.

CARLA. Hadn't been easy. (*To Fern.*) You still got the Brainard Boys?

FERN. Ellen came to fetch 'em half hour ago.

CARLA. Got anymore coming in?

FERN. Not unless they crawl over here on their own.

CARLA. Maple, honey, you got any children?

MAPLE. Nope.

CARLA. You're probably like me, then. I think they're awful cute in the front of a grocery cart, but I'd sooner eat mosquitoes than birth one.

FERN. Carla. Maple wants a baby so badly, she could spit teardrops.

CARLA. Oh, honey, I'm so sorry! Oh, I can't think of anything more tragic than wanting to be a mama and not being able to. Donahue had a woman on the other day, got so whacked out over not being able to have a baby, went out and stole her one, right out of one of those grocery carts, matter-of-fact, but, before she took it, she made pretty dang sure that kid's parents weren't in any shape to come trotting out after her ... Mowed 'em down in the grocery store parking lot ... Tragic ... Tragic ... Who is it has the problem, Maple, honey, you or your husband?

MAPLE. What problem?

CARLA. What I mean is, have you been to see anyone about this?

MAPLE. Well, we ...

CARLA. 'Course, I wouldn't blame you if you hadn't. I haven't been to a gynecologist for years, after hearing about that gynecological cult.

MAPLE. What?!

FERN. Carla, you hear about the damndest things!

CARLA. You didn't hear about that? Women would come into this fellow's office, and after just one appointment, they'd be hooked—brainwashed—give him anything he asked for. And let me tell you, he performed some procedures on those ladies, made a pap smear sound like a picnic.

MAPLE. Good grief!

CARLA. One woman claimed he ...

FERN. Carla! This is one story I'd just as soon go to my grave without hearing.

CARLA. Suit yourself. (*SHE gives them a knowing look.*) So, have you two ever been tested?

MAPLE. Oh, we don't believe in all that testing stuff. Figure it's all in our heads. We just haven't found the key, is all.

CARLA. Is that right? How long you been trying?

MAPLE. 'Bout twelve years.

CARLA. Oh, uh-huh ... (*CARLA gives Fern a look. Pause.*) Guess who I bumped into at the 7-Eleven, guess ... Arnold.

FERN. Palmer? How'd he look?

CARLA. Like he'd just got through swallowing his teeth.

FERN. Poor fellow.

CARLA. I wonder did he notice the microwave yet.

FERN. Shooo ... Probably over there now trying to club himself senseless with a five iron.

(The PHONE rings.)

FERN. Now, this is bound to be Stan. *(Picks up phone.)* Fern's Factory Outlet, how may I help you? ... Oh, hello Mama ... Nope, no relapses. I'd say her jaw is pretty well oiled now. You plannin' on calling every twenty-five minutes today? Oop. There goes your call-us-interrupt-us ... How many time's he called? ... Who's he asking for? ... NO?! ... Mama! ... Mama, don't pick up the phone anymore. That fellow's been calling here too, asking could he speak to Bernice. Called three times ... Well just ... Well just don't ... Just don't pick up the ... Hung up on me. Good night. This is kinda creepy.

CARLA. That fellow called here three times?

FERN. Yeah.

CARLA. Sign of a rapist.

MAPLE. What?!

CARLA. Fellow in Chicago, raped thirty, forty women, always used to call his victims up beforehand, asking could he speak to Hilda. Come to find out later that Hilda was his mean old dead mother, and this was his way of getting even, see. I wouldn't sleep here tonight, Fern, if my life depended on it.

MAPLE. You ever heard of "Bernice's Hair"?

CARLA. That that place out on Walnut, gave me that damned bouffant ... (*CARLA waves her hands around over her head.*)
FERN. No, what she's talking about is a bunch of stars, looks like hair.
MAPLE. It's a constellation up in the sky.
CARLA. You don't say? Hair, up in the sky, huh?... Is it straight or kinky?
FERN. Wouldn't ask that, if I were you.
MAPLE. (*Gives Fern a look.*) Hard to tell.
FERN. What's the point, Maple?
MAPLE. Well, Stan ... thinks ... that ... may be the key.
FERN. Bunch of stars?
MAPLE. Not exactly. It's a kind of theory. Something Stan dreamed up around last Christmas ... He thinks it might help us get pregnant ... Help me get pregnant. Well, you know what I mean.
FERN. No, not exactly, no.
MAPLE. It's just something he dreamed up ... You know Stan. He's always so full of theories.

(*Pause.*)

FERN. Are you gonna tell us what it is?
MAPLE. Well ... See, it all started last Christmas, when I was opening up my presents. Stan says there's one he wants me to save and open last, so, 'course I thought it was gonna be a new washer-dryer, or a microwave, or something like that ...

FERN. Microwave! What time is it?
CARLA. Six fifteen.
FERN. Oh. Sorry, go ahead.
MAPLE. I don't know. It's kinda private.
FERN. Oh no, Maple, I'm sorry, go on.
CARLA. Go ahead, hon. It'll never leave this room.
MAPLE. Well ... It wasn't hardly a microwave.
CARLA. What was it?
MAPLE. Opened it up, pulled out a real, human hair, jet black, wig.

(Pause, while FERN's and CARLA's faces are frozen in anticipation.)

MAPLE. That's exactly how I felt. I tried to freeze my face so it wouldn't move on from the look of surprise it had on it, into what might naturally follow, when Stan says, "Aren't you excited, honey? That's Bernice's Hair. That's gonna be the key to our fertility." I kept my face frozen with some difficulty. (*SHE demonstrates.*) He goes on to say how, maybe the reason we weren't making babies is because somewhere inside of us, we don't believe that Maple can have babies. That Maple is barren. So, if we were to pretend that Maple were someone else, someone like for instance, Bernice with jet black hair, then, well, maybe Bernice could get herself knocked up.

(Pause.)

FERN. Well, I never.
CARLA. Got a unique imagination.
FERN. I'll say ... He have you wear that wig to bed?!
MAPLE. Gosh, Fern, you know we'd do anything to have a baby!
FERN. I guess so! *(Pause.)* Must have been some Christmas.
CARLA. And here we were, stringing popcorn and cranberries.
FERN. Guess it didn't work, did it?
MAPLE. What?
CARLA. The ... theory.
MAPLE. 'Spose it still could.
FERN. You still wearing it?!
MAPLE. Gosh, Fern, you know how desperate we are!
FERN. Desperate, yeah!!
MAPLE. *(Moving over to a corner of the room.)* It's not so bad on. Got it stuffed in this Piggly Wiggly bag. *(SHE digs in the bag and pulls out a sad-looking black wig and puts it on her head.)*
CARLA. Tragic.
FERN. Maple ... How long you two gonna give this wig theory?
MAPLE. I don't know.
FERN. Maple!
MAPLE. We're desperate!
FERN. Yeah, you mentioned that.
CARLA. Tragic.

(Pause.)

MAPLE. I got seven different ones now.
FERN. What?
MAPLE. Yeah ... I'm seven different people now, but for some reason, my name's always Bernice. There's Black-headed Bernice, Blond-headed Bernice, Red-headed Bernice, Brunette Bernice, Long-haired Bernice, Curly-headed Bernice, and ... Bouffant Bernice.
FERN. Bouffant?!!
CARLA. Tragic.
FERN. So, you mean that was Stan calling here asking could he speak to Bernice?! Liked to scare me to death! Why didn't he ask for Maple, so I'd know who the hell he was talking about.

(Pause.
MAPLE looks as if she's going to cry.)

CARLA. I guess it's been a while since he asked for Maple, huh?

(Pause as ALL THREE think about this.)

CARLA. You know all this reminds me of this story I read. It was about this real sick serial murderer, see. Dressed this woman up in six or seven costumes, so when he got around to killing her, it'd be like killing a bunch of different women at the same time. Several birds, you know. Now, when it comes time to commit the crime he figures, why not do it six or seven different ways, see, so that's just what he did, he ... (*Counts on her fingers.*) shot her, stabbed her, strangled her, poisoned her, hung her, and finally, drowned her. Let me see, that's six ... and just generally messed the poor thing up, so you couldn't hardly tell who she'd been in the first place ... ugly.

(The PHONE rings, and the WOMEN stare at it in horror.
On about the fourth ring ARNOLD PALMER pokes his head in the door.)

ARNOLD. Hey there.
ALL THREE WOMEN. AAAHHHHHHHH!

(ARNOLD runs away.
Pause.)

MAPLE. Who was that?
FERN and CARLA. Arnold Palmer.

(LIGHTS fade. End of Scene 2.)

ACT I

Scene 3

LIGHTS come up on FERN and ARNOLD sitting on the couch. FERN is holding a BABY and ARNOLD is holding a Coke. ARNOLD is stunned and answers all of Fern's questions after a slight vacant pause. It is 8:00 p.m. that same day.

FERN. You know, I believe I've seen your wife around, had no idea she was expecting.
ARNOLD. Neither did she, Fern. Thought it was just indigestion or something.
FERN. Well, bless her heart. She must have been pretty excited when she found out it was a real live baby girl, giving her that stomach ache.
ARNOLD. I guess you could say she got pretty excited. But you'd be hitting it a little closer if you'd said irritated.
FERN. Oh ... Your wife doesn't much care for babies?
ARNOLD. Well, I don't believe it was just an oversight on her part to take every stick of furniture but the crib, and the baby in it. 'Course I could be wrong. She could be on some gas station pay phone right now, trying to call me, wondering just exactly what it was she forgot, and could I U.P.S. it over to her, but I wouldn't put money on it ... Yeah, I guess you could say Brenda doesn't much care for babies.

FERN. Sorry to hear that. (*Pause.*) This is one precious little package you got here, one precious little package ...

(*There is an awkward pause as ARNOLD slips back into his thoughts.*)

FERN. (*Screams.*) What on earth you two doing in that bathroom for so long?!

CARLA. (*Popping her head out the bedroom door.*) What?

FERN. What are you doing?

CARLA. Just teaching Maple how to look like Barbie, when you're feeling like G.I. Joe. (*Seeing the baby.*) Oh, isn't she just the thing? Just the sweetest little thing? Say, "I'm just a little baby. Just a teeny-weeny baby." Say, "Who are all these funny-looking, big-headed ladies looking down at me?" Isn't she just the thing? I wouldn't leave you in front of a grocery cart, no siree. I'd never see you again, would I? 'Cause anybody in their right mind would wanna kidnap you.

FERN. Carla!

CARLA. Well, I'll leave you two to talk over your baby business. (*CARLA walks back into the bedroom.*)

FERN. Hey, warn Maple about that bathroom door, would you! (*To Arnold.*) So, what kinda hours are we talking about?

ARNOLD. Welp, I hadn't quite figured that one out yet. I can't say as I've figured anything out yet. I believe my life-style might just be about to make a drastic turnabout, here. (*Thinks about this.*) Yep, drastic's the word that comes to my mind, all right. I might just have to cut out some activities to make room for taking care of a baby.

FERN. Golf?

ARNOLD. Oh, boy, I hadn't thought about ... Hey, how'd you guess I played golf?

FERN. (*Looks at his outfit.*) Seen you practicing your swing in your front yard.

ARNOLD. Didn't think about that, I bet you have ... You ever played yourself?

FERN. Matter-of-fact, yeah, when I was younger. Early twenties, around then. Used to enjoy it too.

ARNOLD. Yeah? What made you quit?

FERN. Uh ... Took up aerobics instead. Don't even have to leave my living room. Comes in handy when you're in the baby watching line. Hey, you might wanna think about that, no sand traps, don't need a caddie. What do you think?

ARNOLD. I guess you took me pretty serious when I mentioned that drastic turnabout. Shoot, I couldn't get outside to air myself once in a while, wouldn't hardly be worth it. May as well just pull the plug.

FERN. That right?

ARNOLD. Yeah, heck, can you imagine being cooped up in here all the time every day? You'd for sure start to go kinda barky.

FERN. Barky?

ARNOLD. Like a penned-up dog. Barky ... (*HE twirls his finger around his ear.*) Arf, arf ...

THE VIEW FROM HERE 39

Friend of mine had a mother didn't leave her house for six – seven years, something like that, claims she turned the color of a manila envelope.

FERN. Manila envelope, huh?

ARNOLD. See, there's a vitamin you get from the sun. Couldn't tell you which one it was, but you don't get it, your body will just start to rot. (*Pause.*) You know, Fern, I got a confession to make.

FERN. What's that?

ARNOLD. I don't know the first thing about taking care of a baby.

FERN. You never watched your wife with her?

ARNOLD. Brenda didn't exactly encourage a feeling of unity there toward the end.

FERN. Oh, I'm sorry.

ARNOLD. So am I, Fern, so am I ... Guess this old dog'll be learning some new tricks, huh?

FERN. Guess so.

(*PHONE rings.*)

FERN. Oh boy.

(*THE PHONE continues to ring and FERN smiles weakly at Arnold. CARLA and MAPLE come running out of the bedroom. CARLA has a curling iron in Maple's hair, so THEY appear attached. ALL THREE WOMEN stare at the phone. ARNOLD stares at the women, wondering why no one is answering the phone. FERN looks up at Maple. MAPLE shakes her head, no. THEY all look at the phone.*)

FERN. Suppose it could be Mama. *(SHE answers the phone.)* Fern's ... Flat Bed Trucks, how may I help you? ... *(FERN's eyes widen, and SHE looks at Maple, finally pinches her nose to alter her voice.)* Sorry wrong number! *(SHE slams the phone down. Pause.)* How's that Coke coming along, Arnold? Can I get you another?

ARNOLD. Oh, no, This will do me fine, thank you. I'm just fine .... 'Cept for ... my name's not Arnold.

FERN. Oh, I'm so sorry, I keep doing that. It's just you remind me of someone I used to know, name was Arnold, dressed a lot like you.

ARNOLD. How's that?

FERN. Looked! ... a lot like you ... Name was Arnold ... Wpheu! Smells like someone's grilling their kitty cats.

CARLA and MAPLE. *(Discovering it is Maple's hair.)* AAAHHHHHHHH!

(THEY run back into the bedroom. Pause.)

FERN. You don't mind if I turn on the T.V., do you? I'll keep the sound down. I'm entered in a raffle out at the Super Kroger's. Brand new microwave.

ARNOLD. That right, huh? *(Pause.)* Microwave, huh? *(ARNOLD looks miserably toward his house and slips back into his thoughts.)* I guess you'd call it an eating disorder, what she had. She'd get a little agitated and, bang!—her mouth would pop open and something would get jammed in there. Some of the strangest derned stuff you'd ever wanna put in your mouth, too. Shoot ... Combinations of things. Strange combinations of things ... It wouldn't do for her just to eat a bag of Oreos, she'd have to dip 'em in peanut butter or grape jelly, or some such thing. Watched her finish off a whole jar of mayonnaise, one time, dipping pickles. Shoooee. She was fast too, didn't hardly look like she chewed ... And she'd always want to eat the last thing she saw advertised on the T.V. She'd send me out for the craziest dern things ... Little Debbie's ... Fluff ... Count Chocula. Sometimes I'd have to go to two or three different stores, just to find what she wanted ... You ever know anyone with an eating disorder?

FERN. Mama had a thing where she'd spit up anytime she ate and watched something exciting on the T.V. at the same time. Is that a disorder?

ARNOLD. I don't believe so, I believe that's just ... Oh, I don't know about all that stuff. Disorders, phobias ... Seems like people get a little confused, read some crazy article in a magazine and claim it fits 'em to a T, so they join up, slap a label on themselves.

(Pause as they BOTH think about this.)

ARNOLD. Brenda was unhappy, what it was ... just plain unhappy. (*ARNOLD presses his eyes for a moment.*)

FERN. I'm sorry.
ARNOLD. So am I, Fern. So am I ...
FERN. You have any idea she was taking off today?
ARNOLD. Shoot, Sherlock would have been fooled. Kinda thing that could bust your mind apart, never be the same.
FERN. What do you mean?
ARNOLD. Heck, you'd have seen me when I walked back in that house today ... Tell you what, Fern, there's nothing scarier on this earth than feeling your mind start to split apart. Not a blessed thing scarier.

(Pause while BOTH of them think about this.)

FERN. What did it feel like?
ARNOLD. Kinda hard to explain.
FERN. Like the earth dive-bombed into another part of space, and your shoes weren't sticky enough to hold you on?
ARNOLD. *(Pause.)* Yeah.
FERN. Let it go.
ARNOLD. What?
FERN. That feeling. Just let it go right now. Won't do you a bit of good.
ARNOLD. I can see what you're ...
FERN. You let it have it's way, it'll cripple you, see. So just put it behind you. Put it behind you and keep moving. Believe me. You can't move forward, long as you're busy pointing at the past. *(Pause. FERN smiles shyly.)* Listen to me ...

Boy, you must need some breathing time, huh. How about I take care of the baby while you go back home and collect yourself.

ARNOLD. Well, shoot, Fern, I ... I don't know if I ...

FERN. Go ahead.

ARNOLD. Gosh, that's awful nice of you. Gosh, I ... Well, I could stand to make a few calls, that sort of thing.

FERN. You take your time. Me and this little girl will get to know each other.

ARNOLD. Awful nice of you, Fern. I sure do appreciate this ... You know which house is mine?

FERN. The one with the front yard looks like a golf green?

ARNOLD. That's the one, yeah. Drilled a hole in it, too, practice my putting ... Yeah ... O.K., be back soon. I sure do appreciate this.

(HE walks out and FERN watches him walk away for a moment before CARLA enters.)

CARLA. Where'd Arnold go?

FERN. Home.

CARLA. Home? What for? Skate around in his socks? ... Think he's gonna pull through?

FERN. Yeah, he just needs to keep moving. Get through today and keep moving.

CARLA. That right, huh?

FERN. Yeah, yeah, I've had that figured out up here for years ... (*Points to her head.*) It's the rest of me's hard of hearing.

(Pause.)

CARLA. Read somewhere, where this fellow's head was completely severed from his body, and he went on to live for two more hours.

FERN. Is that right?

CARLA. Yep. Talking from one end, passing gas from the other. (*Slight pause.*) Oh, will you look at that little thing? Can I hold her? (*Takes baby.*) Will you just look at that precious little thing?

FERN. You tell Maple about that bathroom door?

CARLA. (*To baby.*) Say, "I'm just a precious little thing." Say, "Who's that big old head, looking down at me?" Say, "That must be Carla from up the street, with that big old head of hers."

FERN. (*Looking at the T.V.*) Look here, they're getting ready for that raffle out at the Super Kroger's. (*FERN turns the T.V. up.*)

T.V. ANNOUNCER. And the young lady picking the lucky ticket today is Miss Melba Shaw, from our Meat and Poultry Department.

FERN. Pick it, Melba!

T.V. ANNOUNCER. And how are you today, Melba?

MELBA. Just fine, thank you, and happy to be here on the T.V.

T.V. ANNOUNCER. Isn't that nice. Folks, after Melba announces our lucky winner today, she'll be waiting here, out at the Super Kroger's for

exactly one hour. If, after one hour, the winner has not claimed his or her microwave, we'll be selecting another ticket.
FERN. Sounds fair to me.

(There is a loud BANGING coming from the direction of the bathroom.)

CARLA. What's that banging?
FERN. *(Glued to the T.V.)* I believe it's Maple, locked herself in the bathroom.
T.V. ANNOUNCER. And the winner is ...
FERN. *(Throws herself to her knees.)* Please please please ...
MELBA. Miss Fern Arbor, 712 Glen Oaks Drive.

(FERN jumps around the room, while CARLA puts the baby in one of the cribs and moves closer to the T.V.)

FERN. AAAAAAHHHHHHHHH!!! Thank you, thank you, thank you, thank you, thank you, thank you, thank you, thank you! *(SHE is running around the living room, jumping up and down on the furniture. SHE dances around with her stuffed animals.)* I'M A WINNER!! Me, Fern Arbor, a winner!!! Thank you, thank you, thank you!
CARLA. Fern.
FERN. *(FERN runs in the bedroom.)* Maple, I won a microwave! *(SHE runs back out. The*

BANGING picks up.) AAAAAAAAHHHHHH! A microwave! Thank you, thank you, thank you ...

CARLA. (*A little louder this time.*) Fern!

FERN. Thank you! Thank you, thank you thank you thank you thank you ...

CARLA. FERN!!

FERN. WHAT!!!

CARLA. They're saying you have to appear in person to claim it, Fern. Appear in person, out at the Super Kroger's.

FERN. (*Mouthing the words, but no sound is coming out.*) Oh my God ... Oh my God ... O ... My ... God ... (*SHE wanders around the room, trying to find a place that is comfortable, which is impossible. Finding her voice.*) Super Kroger's ... Super Kroger's ... I've never even seen a Super Kroger's. They came after I ... Oh ... My ... God ... Oh ... My ... God. (*SHE tries to find comfortable positions on the couch. SHE leans over from the back of the couch, so that her head is on the seat and her feet are in the air.*) Oh My God ... Oh My God ... (*Pulling herself up.*) Carla, you have to go!

CARLA. Fern, you know I can't drive on the new moon.

FERN. Carla!

CARLA. Fern!

FERN. Maple, don't tell me you're locked in that bathroom!

MAPLE. (*Offstage.*) I'm locked in the bathroom!

FERN. Of all the ... (*Looks at Carla.*) Carla?!!

CARLA. Fern!
FERN. *(SHE digs around under the couch and pulls out something.)* Read this.
CARLA. What is it?
FERN. My old driver's license. *(Hands it to her.)*
CARLA. 5 feet, 5 inches. 115 lbs. Brunette. Shit, Fern.
FERN. If you were a brunette, they might overlook the rest.

(THEY both look at the Piggly Wiggly bag.)

CARLA. Fern, you're not ...
FERN. *(Yelling to Maple.)* Maple?! You sure you can't budge that door?!
MAPLE. *(Offstage.)* Won't budge!

(FERN runs over to the bag and dumps the wigs on the floor. THEY stare at them for a moment, FERN holds up a wig.)

FERN. Here.
CARLA. Fern, put that back, you don't know where that's been!
FERN. Carla, please?
CARLA. Fern!
FERN. *(Throwing herself at her feet.)* Please, please, please, please?!
CARLA. Get up.

(FERN gets up.)

CARLA. Give it here!

(FERN hands her the wig and CARLA holds it at arm's length in her fingers as if it were alive.

CARLA. Oh, ooky! (*SHE throws it away.*) You've got to go yourself.
FERN. Oh my God, oh my God, oh my God ... You take me?
CARLA. I CAN'T DRIVE ON THE NEW MOON!
FERN. Mama! (*Runs to phone and dials.*) Come on Mama ... Please be there, Mama ... Pick up the phone, Mama ... I told Mama not to pick up the phone!!! (*Slams the phone down.*) What am I gonna do? ... What am I gonna do? ...
CARLA. Run over, get Arnold to take you.
FERN. Arnold, good idea! ... (*SHE runs to the screen door and just touches the handle, and pulls her hand back.*) OH MY GOD! (*SHE runs over to the couch and jumps straight up and down on it.*) Oh boy, oh boy, oh boy, oh boy, oh boy, oh boy, oh boy. (*SHE takes a few practice runs at the door and finally runs out the door.*) AAAAAAAAHHHHHHHH!!!!!!! ...

(The sound of her screaming trails away, as we hear the BANGING in the bathroom getting louder.
Pause.)

CARLA. Damn.

ACT II

Scene 1

Just before the LIGHTS come up we hear MAPLE singing. SHE should be singing something inappropriate for a baby. When the LIGHTS come up SHE is found alone, dancing around with the BABY. It is later on that same night.

MAPLE. (*To baby.*) You know, if I were a different sort of person, the sort that gets on the "Phil Donahue Show," we'd be halfway to Quebec by now. But, I'd be smarter than those women on the Donahue Show. I wouldn't get caught. We'd settle down in some town up there, and I'd get my face rearranged and we'd live in a little house without a single stick of furniture. 'Cause somewhere in that little soul of yours, you'd have the feeling that someone, way back, thought more of their matching Tupperware furniture than they did of you. Maybe you wouldn't remember it that way, but there'd just be this little feeling, see, so we wouldn't have even one stick of furniture, just to ease your mind. How's that sound, baby?

(The PHONE rings and MAPLE walks over to it.)

MAPLE. Stop it! (*It keeps ringing and SHE touches it, then takes her hand away.*) Stop it, stop it, stop it, stop it!!!

(*It stops ringing. FERN walks in the screen door, and stands there with a vacant, terrorized look.*)

MAPLE. Fern? You O.K?

(*FERN opens her mouth to speak but nothing comes out.*)

MAPLE. Well, did you get it? ... Did you get the microwave?

(*FERN looks back out the door.*)

MAPLE. Is Arnold bringing it in?
ARNOLD. (*Entering with a microwave box.*) Where is it you want this, Fern?
MAPLE. I wish you'd look! ... You can set it down anywhere, Arnold.
ARNOLD. Boy, I guess I'd better get used to being called Arnold.
MAPLE. Well, Good Lord, Fern, how'd you do? How'd it feel?

(*FERN holds her head.*)

MAPLE. You wanna sit down? Can I get you a drink, or something?

ARNOLD. I guess it's not every day you win a microwave out at the Super Kroger's.

MAPLE. You look kinda green, Fern, how about it?

ARNOLD. Yeah, a drink sounds pretty good. Give Arnold here one too.

MAPLE. There's some whisky out in the kitchen, Arnold, would you mind grabbing that for us.

ARNOLD. Not a bit. (*HE heads toward the kitchen.*)

MAPLE. Fern, you sure you don't want to lie down or something?

(*FERN looks blankly at Maple.*)

MAPLE. You're not gonna spill your cookies out here in the living room are you?

(*FERN makes a sick face and turns away.*)

ARNOLD. (*Entering.*) Boy, I don't believe I've ever seen anybody win a prize before. Well, nothing important, you know. Watched Brenda win a Big Mac once, didn't even faze her.

MAPLE. Mama won a Big Mac and some fries one time, thought she was gonna detonate, she got so excited.

ARNOLD. Well, I guess that's one way Fern here doesn't take after your mama.

MAPLE. How's that?

ARNOLD. Fern acted more like she was going to a funeral, than picking up a prize. Isn't that right, Fern? (*Slight pause.*) Yes ma'am, just as calm as death. You'd of seen her coming down the aisle, you'd of thought she was just stopping in for a can of tuna and a magazine.

(FERN looks at Arnold with a kind of wonder.)

ARNOLD. 'Cept for she kept her ears plugged up with her fingers the whole time. Yep, 'cept for her fingers in her ears, and that old pair of sunglasses she dug out of my glove compartment, you'd have thought she came in every day to the Super Kroger's to claim prizes. Then there was that lady ... What was her name, Fern? ... Melba, that was it. Shoot, that Melba was one strange ranger. Anyway, there's Melba expecting some wired up housewife to come screaming down the aisles, when up crawls Fern here, looking like she'd come in for a root canal.
MAPLE. Poor Fern.
ARNOLD. Melba looks at Fern and says, "Ma'am?" and Fern gives me a little kick in the back of my shoe. I figure that's her way of saying, "Jump on in, Arnold, say something." So I say, "This is Fern Arbor come to claim her microwave." And that's when Melba starts acting kinda odd ...
MAPLE. How odd?
ARNOLD. Turns her back on us, and starts waving and pointing at us back over her shoulder,

like this. (*ARNOLD demonstrates by turning upstage and waving and pointing over his shoulder.*) That was our view of it. Then she turns back around, (*ARNOLD turns back around facing downstage.*) and says in a kind of whisper, without hardly moving her lips, "I'm sorry, sir, what was it you said?" So I say it again, just like I'd been asked to memorize it from the first time, "This is Fern Arbor come to claim her microwave." Well that seemed to spin old Melba around again. (*ARNOLD spins around upstage.*) And she says in a kinda pinched up high voice, "Well, Miss Fern Arbor, this must be your lucky day! Can you tell us how it feels to be the lucky winner of a brand new microwave?" And she sticks her hand out in the direction of the microwave, and watches it for a minute, like it's alive. Then she gives us the front of her again, (*ARNOLD spins around facing downstage.*) and I look over at Fern and say, "She's thrilled to death." And that's when Fern here figures she's had enough, I guess.

MAPLE. Uh-oh, what'd she do?

ARNOLD. Jammed her wallet in my hand, whispers something about Co-co Puffs, and bolts.

MAPLE. Bolts?

ARNOLD. Yeah, guess all the excitement finally got to her ... When I got out to the car, found her rolled up in a ball in the back seat, with a sweater over her head.

MAPLE. (*Pats Fern.*) Poor Fern.

ARNOLD. She's been kinda froze up ever since. Probably thaw out in a minute with this. (*Indicates with his drink.*)

MAPLE. Fern, you O.K.? You wanna lie down or something?

(*Pause.*)

FERN. (*As if it had just occurred to her.*) I think maybe I'll just ... lie down ... (*FERN stares at Maple and doesn't move. Pause.*) How'd you get out of the bathroom?

MAPLE. Carla burned me out with her curling iron.

FERN. Oh.

MAPLE. I don't believe it'll jam up on you again, Fern.

FERN. Yeah ... Where is Carla?

MAPLE. She ran home to listen to the police scanner. Said she'd probably have to be the one to identify you after they scraped you up off the highway. (*Pause.*) Fern, you don't look too perky to me, sure you don't want to lie down?

(*Pause.*)

FERN. (*Again, as if it had just occurred to her.*) I think maybe I'll just ... lie down ... (*SHE still doesn't appear to move. Turns to Arnold.*) Thank you, Arnold.

ARNOLD. Heck, I wouldn't have missed that to meet the president, Fern, that was big fun, I tell you what.

FERN. Well, I think maybe I'll just ... lie down. (*SHE stands up, looks out blankly, and walks into the bedroom.*)

ARNOLD. Welp, guess I'll get going, let you two get some shut eye. (*ARNOLD moves to get the baby.*)

MAPLE. Didn't I hear your wife took all your furniture, Arnold?

ARNOLD. (*Taking the baby from Maple.*) She sure did, Maple. (*To baby.*) Guess we don't have to worry about tripping over anything, do we, sweetheart?

MAPLE. Well goodness, why don't you and the baby spend the night out here in the living room? I can't stand to think of you two over there in that empty old house.

ARNOLD. Gosh, Maple, you've already done so much, I ...

MAPLE. (*Reaches under the couch and pulls out a pillow and a blanket.*) I'll just climb in with Fern tonight, won't bother us a bit.

ARNOLD. Gosh that's awful nice of you ... shoot.

MAPLE. Guess we'd all better get some sleep before that little milk alarm goes off. (*SHE moves to the bedroom door.*)

ARNOLD. Gosh this is awful generous.

MAPLE. (*Stops at the door and turns to Arnold.*) I'm sorry about your wife, Arnold.

ARNOLD. Oh, gosh, Maple, I—well thank you for—I tell you, I don't know what I'd have done without your sister and you being so—She was unhappy, what it was ... just plain unhappy.

MAPLE. Don't know what it is makes people run away, when they should be running toward.

ARNOLD. You and me both, Maple. You and me both.

(Pause.)

MAPLE. I think maybe I'll just unplug the phone for tonight. What do you think. Hate to wake the baby. (*Unplugs phone.*) Night, night. (*SHE moves into the bedroom and shuts the door.*)

ARNOLD. Night. (*HE watches the door for a moment.*) Gosh, that's nice. (*To baby.*) I guess you and me are two lucky ducks, eh, baby? Look here, I got a nice comfy couch to sleep on, and shoot, you have your choice of three, count 'em, three cribs. I guess we're just about as lucky as they come, huh ... (*Pause as HE stares out into space.*) Your mama was unhappy, what it was, sweetheart, just plain unhappy ... (*HE shakes off his feelings and looks down at the baby again.*) Shoot, you musta been born under some special star, baby. Look at what happened to you today, you lost one friend and already you've found two more to replace her. You're gonna have a charmed life, little one ... a charmed life ... (*HE looks up.*) A charmed life ... (*HE starts to cry and presses his eyes with his fingers.*)

(LIGHTS fade. End of Scene 1.)

ACT II

Scene 2

LIGHTS come up on ARNOLD, FERN, and MAPLE sprawled out in the room, exhausted after a night with the baby. MAPLE holds the baby. It is 9:00 the following morning.

FERN. *(After a moment.)* Guess she just felt a little funny in a new crib.
ARNOLD. You mean every night's not going to be like last night, Fern?
FERN. I believe in that case, Arnold, we'd have to kill her.

(Pause while THEY all think about this.)

FERN. That was a joke.
MAPLE. Still, it makes you think twice about running off to Canada and having your face rearranged.

(FERN and ARNOLD are too exhausted to ask what this means.)

MAPLE. (*Looks down at the baby.*) Look at her now, nine o'clock in the morning and she's just as peaceful as a pond.

(*Pause while MAPLE looks at the baby, and FERN and ARNOLD let their heads roll back and close their eyes. Suddenly CARLA comes bursting through the front door.*)

CARLA. Fern! Fern! You're never gonna believe this! Guess who I just saw on the early morning news? Guess. And get this, wearing a scary pair of shades, with her fingers in her ears! Now can you guess? There's Arnold, saying, "This is Fern Arbor, come to claim her microwave." Hooey! That just about pushed me over the edge, I'll tell you what! There you were on my T.V.! My friend, Fern, on the T.V.! Damn, I'd wished I'd had the guts to drive you over to the Super Kroger's last night! Oooo, I wish to goodness I'd had the balls to do that! I'd have been on the T.V.! Damn! Oooo, I could just about kick myself, I could ... 'Course if I'd driven you, we'd probably be wrapped around some telephone pole, in a dead coma ... But damn, that was a religious experience seeing you on the T.V. Damn!!!

(*SHE catches her breath, and the PHONE rings. ALL THREE WOMEN stare at it, with a glazed look.
Pause as the PHONE continues to ring.*)

MAPLE. Who plugged the phone back in?
ARNOLD. Uh, I plugged the phone in.

(ALL THREE WOMEN stare at Arnold. Pause. The PHONE continues to ring.)

FERN. Arnold, would you mind getting that for me?
ARNOLD. No. No, wouldn't mind a bit.
FERN. If he's asking for anyone besides Fern or Maple here, you can just tell him to try another number.
ARNOLD. Okey dokey. *(Picks up the phone.)* Hello? ... uh ... *(Looks at Fern.)* This is ... Arnold from across the street. *(Back at Fern.)* Palmer?

(FERN nods her head yes.)

ARNOLD. *(Flattered, back to phone.)* Yeah.
FERN. Is that Mama?
ARNOLD. Fern wants to know, is this Mama?
FERN. Here, I'll take that, Arnold, I appreciate it. *(Takes the phone. Holding the phone away from her ear.)* Mama ... Mama, settle down ... Yeah, Carla just ran over, said she saw it too. *(Holds the phone away again.)* Mama! Mama, you're gonna bust if you're not careful ... Yeah, that was Arnold with me ... Well, it's a long story. Maple was locked in the bathroom and ... Now, don't get your panties in knots. Carla burned her out ... I'm not gonna tell you anymore,

until you can get a grip on yourself ... (*Getting upset.*) No, Mama! That is not what it means! So you can just forget it! Forget it ever happened! ... (*Controlling herself.*) Now, do this for me right now. Lean over front-ways and get some blood to your head. Are you doing what I told you? ... Mama? ... Mama? ... You there? ... (*SHE puts the phone face up on the table.*)

ARNOLD. She O.K.?

FERN. Fainted.

ARNOLD. Is anybody there with her?

FERN. Oh, she'll be O.K. Happens all the time, when she leans over front-ways ... I figure it's better she faints than has a stroke, so I tell her to lean over front-ways, get some blood to her head. When she comes out of it, she can never remember what it was made her faint. Doesn't take but a minute.

(*Pause as THEY all stare at the phone.*)

CARLA. Boy, I know just how your mama feels. I got so worked up running back and forth between my police scanner and my T.V. this morning, set off my dog-barking machine.

FERN. What?

ARNOLD. What's a dog-barking machine?

CARLA. You've never heard of a dog-barking machine?

ARNOLD. No, what's it do??

CARLA. (*Slight pause.*) Barks like a dog.

ARNOLD. Barks like a dog, huh?

CARLA. Yeah, barks like a dog. Keeps away burglars ... I didn't want little poopies all over my yard so I got me one of those dog barking machines. Fern, I'm gonna have to get you one of those. Everyone aughta have one. Maple, Arnold, everyone. (*Pause.*) Anyway, when I ran home last night, I turned on my scanner and my T.V. at the same time, see ...

(*The PHONE starts screaming.*)

CARLA. Got so wore out juggling my brain back and forth between the two of 'em, fell asleep right there on my living room couch, both machines blaring away. Woke up this morning with the most God-awful—What in the ... ?

FERN. (*Picks the phone up.*) Mama. Mama, calm down ... Well, that didn't do you a damn bit of good, did it? ... Nope ... nope, I'm not gonna tell you one more word about it 'til you can iron yourself out ... Nope ... Nope ... Now, Mama ... No. I'll call you later. (*Hangs up.*) What were you saying, Carla?

CARLA. Well, before I could turn off my scanner I just had to hear what was going on. Can't resist that thing. Get this. Officer pulls this fellow over for speeding out on Cherokee Parkway, walks up to the car window, fellow's wearing a big blond wig, like a woman would wear.

ARNOLD. You're kidding?

CARLA. When he asks the fellow why it was he was going 75 in a 55 mile an hour speed zone, fellow says, he's out looking for his wife.
ARNOLD. (*Laughing.*) Shooeee ... Takes all kinds ...

(*MAPLE looks a little green.*)

CARLA. I guess it does ... Anyway, it was about that time I happened to look over at the T.V., and there's my friend Fern at the Super Krogers ...
MAPLE. Big, like bouffant?
CARLA. Lord, I wouldn't doubt it, Maple.
ARNOLD. It's a wild world out there.
CARLA. I tell you what!
FERN. (*Who has been watching Maple.*) Is Bouffant Bernice a blond?
MAPLE. Bleached.
CARLA. (*Finally getting it.*) Good Lord, you don't think ... Good God ...
ARNOLD. What did they do with him?
CARLA. Took him in. Thought he might be disturbed.
MAPLE. (*Looking lost.*) Disturbed ? ...
ARNOLD. I'd say that's a pretty fair description.
FERN. I wonder if we should call down to the police station, Maple?
MAPLE. (*Still lost.*) Disturbed ...

(*The PHONE rings, and MAPLE gasps.*

THE VIEW FROM HERE 63

Pause, as it continues to ring.)

ARNOLD. You want me to get that, Fern?

FERN. No thanks, Arnold, I'd better get it this time. (*Picks up phone.*) Fern's Filling Station, how may I help you? ... Oh, I'm sorry officer this really isn't a filling station, that's just a little joke ... Uh huh ... Oh, I was afraid of that ... No, actually her name's Maple, but that's another story. Does he want to talk to her? ... O.K. well, let me see if I can get her. (*SHE covers the receiver with her hand.*) Maple, you up to this?

MAPLE. They're calling him disturbed?

FERN. That may be what the police are calling him, but we've always known him as Stan .... The question is, are you gonna get on this phone and talk to your husband or not?

MAPLE. Disturbed.

FERN. (*FERN's hand drops away from the receiver.*) Now, you're not gonna let some fat-headed public servant sum up in twelve seconds the man you've been married to for the past twelve years, are you? (*Realizing the officer has probably heard this.*) Sorry, officer, just trying to make a point here. (*SHE covers the phone with her hand. To Maple.*) What do you say?

MAPLE. Maybe I'd better talk to him, huh?

FERN. I believe that'd be the best thing. (*In the phone.*) Yeah, officer, she'll talk to him.

MAPLE. (*Taking the phone.*) Stan, honey, you there? ... Hello, baby ... You O.K., honey? ... Oh, Stan ... Oh, I'm so sorry ... Oh, honey, I'm so sorry you have to go through this ... (*SHE starts to cry.*) I believe you just need a rest is all. They'll let you just rest in there ... Yes, I know, honey. We just let ourselves get too worked up over trying to make babies, is all ... What's that? ... (*SHE is getting more hysterical.*) No! Don't you ever believe that! You are not disturbed, just tired. Just tired is all ... I'm on my way down there right now, sweetheart. You wait for me and don't be scared ... I know ... I love you too, honey. Don't be scared. Don't be scared, my angel ... (*SHE hangs up the phone, pauses, and looks at the baby.*) You must think we're pretty silly, huh. We get all twisted around and stupid trying to make little things like you, and you just pop into the world like it was as easy as making toast. (*To the others.*) I'd better get down to the station, sign those papers. (*To Fern.*) Fern, I could sure use a hand to hold. You think, after last night? ...

FERN. (*Shocked.*) Maple I ... I don't know, I ... (*FERN stands for a moment looking lost, SHE walks across the room and gets her wallet. Walks back across to the door. Looks at it for a moment. Touches the handle and pulls her hand away covering her mouth. Turns back to Maple.*) I just ... I just can't, Maple.

(*Slight pause.*)

CARLA. Here, I'll go with you, Maple.
FERN. (*Quietly.*) I'm sorry.

(CARLA puts her arm around MAPLE and starts to lead her out.)

CARLA. You know, I read an article about our local loony bin, not too long ago, and they were saying how it was clean as a whistle and as cheerful as Christmas. Said the Queen of England would feel at home in there ...

(THEY are out the door.)

FERN. *(Watching them leave, with her head against the door.)* God, I'm so sorry ... I'm so sorry ... So sorry ...
ARNOLD. *(Watching Fern.)* How long had it been, Fern?
FERN. Hm?
ARNOLD. How long had it been since you went out that door?
FERN. June 13, 1979.

(Pause.)

ARNOLD. Must have been some night for you last night, huh.
FERN. Last night was nothing! It didn't mean a thing. It doesn't mean a thing. I'll know. I'll know when it's time ... I'll know.

(Pause.)

ARNOLD. When I was in the third grade, I had something where ... Well, we lived out on a farm, see, and I had to walk down a long driveway, meet the school bus. There was a big kid, eighth-grader, used to pick the bus up there too. One morning, this kid got it in his head to restructure my face with his boots, and left me to crawl back down the driveway to Mama. The next day Mama thought maybe she'd walk with me to meet the bus, only we got about ten feet down the driveway before I stopped. Mama held her hand out to me and said, (*HE demonstrates.*) "Can you go any further?" and I said, "No, Mama, I just can't." (*Slight pause as HE watches Fern.*) Well, we ... we turned around and walked back inside. The day after that we headed out again, only this time I got about twenty-five feet before I stopped. Mama held her hand out to me just like she did before and asked, (*Again HE demonstrates.*) "Can you go any further?" I said, "No Mama," so we turned around and went back inside. Well, it was about a week later before we made it to the end of that driveway ... You know what Mama said to me when we got there, Fern?

(*FERN turns to him.*)

ARNOLD. She said, "It takes an awful big man to know his own heart as well as you know yours."

(*Pause.*)

FERN. Said your wife took your microwave, Arnold?
ARNOLD. She sure did, Fern.
FERN. Why don't you take that one on over to your house this morning. I never did much care for a microwave.

(FERN walks into her bedroom and shuts the door. ARNOLD watches the door for a moment before HE walks over to the baby and picks her up. HE finally walks out the front door with the BABY.)

(LIGHTS fade. End of Scene 2.)

ACT II

Scene 3

It is 9:00 PM on the Fourth of July, four weeks later. LIGHTS come up on the empty room for a moment. Two additions to the room, are Arnold's golf bag and a dog-barking machine. FERN comes out of the bedroom, pulling on high-heeled shoes. SHE has a dress on and appears to be dressed to go out. SHE is very nervous. SHE slams around the room looking for an earring or lipstick, some last minute touch, before SHE finally notices the baby in one of the cribs.

FERN. What are you looking at? 'Course, I'm scared. It's just not safe around here anymore. Wish I'd never heard of that stupid raffle! (*Moves around the room and looks back at baby.*) Boy, you've got a piercing stare. I was in shock that night. Adrenalin was all it was. Ever heard of adrenalin? Everybody assumes that was the cure, and I should be downtown shouting alleluia in the middle of J.C. Penny's. Shit!!! (*Pause.*) (*Looks back at baby.*) You know, I never have worked out whether it's kinda nutty to talk to babies or not. I mean, you're alive but ... There's a good chance you're not sucking up too much of what I'm saying.

(The PHONE rings and FERN picks it up.)

FERN. Fern's ... ah hell ... Hello, Mama ... Yeah, well this time I'm really gonna go, got a dress on and everything. (*SHE paces nervously.*) It's just a matter of driving out, watching the fireworks, and driving back. Don't even have to get out of the car. I'll be fine, just fine. Worry about the house being robbed when I'm gone, don't worry about me ... That was ... That was a joke, Mama ... Well, if it makes you feel better, I'll plug in my new dog-barking machine, it'll be safe as aspirin. (*SHE plugs in the dog-barking machine.*) Huh? ... Barks like a dog ... Yeah, barks like a dog.

(We hear ARNOLD and CARLA laughing as THEY approach the door.)

FERN. Oh, I gotta go, Mama. Call you in the morning.

(SHE hangs up the phone, and runs back into her bedroom. CARLA and ARNOLD enter.)

ARNOLD. Hey, Fern!
FERN. (*Offstage.*) Be right out!

(CARLA makes herself comfortable on the couch and picks up a magazine as ARNOLD moves to the baby.)

ARNOLD. (*HE picks the baby up out of the crib.*) How's my baby girl this evening? Show Daddy those soft pink teeth of yours ... There's a girl ... (*HE keeps the baby in one arm as HE pulls a putter out of his golf bag with the other. HE pulls a ball from his pocket and begins to putt.*)
CARLA. (*Watches him for a moment.*) Did you know that golf is the upset of 20% of your failed marriages in the United States? ... Fellow in this very magazine, couple of issues back, spent so much time practicing his swing, claims he lost the ability to lift his arms out sideways—armpits fused—nearly ruined him.

ARNOLD. What do you mean?

CARLA. Like this. (*SHE stands up with her arms glued to her sides, flapping her hands.*)

ARNOLD. No, I mean, what did he do where something like that would ruin him?

CARLA. I can't exactly remember, Arnold, but I believe he was working himself up in a career that involved a lot of this. (*SHE waves her arms around in the air.*)

ARNOLD. (*Letting her wave awhile.*) Is that right?

CARLA. I read it right here in this very magazine, couple of months back.

ARNOLD. Uh huh ...

(*SHE sits back down and opens her magazine. Pause.*)

ARNOLD. Airport job, maybe.

CARLA. (*Gives him a stony look.*) When was the last time you were out to the golf course?

ARNOLD. I don't feel right leaving Fern alone here with the baby.

CARLA. She's not gonna go out there with you.

ARNOLD. Oh, I don't know about that.

CARLA. I'd back off, I were you, Arnold. She's good and fused, like an angry wart, you pick at it too much, just gets uglier.

ARNOLD. How do you figure she's gonna get out that door, then.

CARLA. Oh, I always assumed it'd be a tragedy that'd do it. House burns down ... Or better yet, some poor little kid gets hit by a truck, right outside her house. Maybe it's a kid she used to take care of, see. Little thing's out there twitching, just barely alive, and Fern's the only one that sees it. It's a hit and run, see. Kid's flat out in the middle of the road, when here comes another truck, big as a tank this time, barreling down the road. It's curtains for that kid if she doesn't run out to stop it. Fern's screaming, throwing herself against the door. Truck's getting closer. Kid's just a little bloody smudge in the road, truck'll never see it. It's getting closer, Closer! CLOSER!

ARNOLD. Carla.

CARLA. Hey, what did you do back there, Fern?! Hang yourself?!

ARNOLD. Carla, this is a life were talking about here, not some splashy tabloid.

CARLA. What's that supposed to mean?

ARNOLD. Big Foot's not going to stick his hairy head in here and scare her out the house.

CARLA. What do you think, she's gonna walk out the door on her own? Check the length of her grass? Wave to the neighbors?

ARNOLD. Can't think of anything simpler.

CARLA. Fellow on the news other day, had him a wife like that, got so frustrated, tried smoking her out ...

ARNOLD. Carla ...

CARLA. But the plan backfired on him, to put it lightly, in the most God-awful, ugly tragedy you ever ...

ARNOLD. Carla!

(Pause.)

CARLA. Ok, ok. So it's fireworks this time, huh?
ARNOLD. Yeah.
CARLA. Well, take my advice and keep your heart zipped up in your chest where it belongs.
ARNOLD. Why do you say that?
CARLA. She's gonna come out swinging, Arnold, and I'm not sure how much more of this you can take.

(Pause.
MAPLE walks up the sidewalk humming to herself.)

MAPLE. *(Entering.)* Is she ready?
ARNOLD. She's back there getting dressed right now. I'd better run, get me some long pants on. *(HE hands the baby to MAPLE.)* Keep her courage up, till I can get back.
MAPLE. You got it.

(ARNOLD leaves.)

CARLA. Fern, what in the hell are you doing back there?!

(FERN creeps out of the bedroom, SHE is dressed more completely now, with earrings, and a little make-up.)

CARLA. Get a load of you!
FERN. Arnold left?
MAPLE. Went to change.
FERN. Oh.
CARLA. Arnold made a pass yet?
FERN. Carla.
CARLA. He's been sleeping on your couch for a month now, what hell else is he s'posed to do? ... I hope he's not waiting for the divorce to come through, we'll all be dead.
MAPLE. Fern, you are photo pretty in that little frock ... Oooo, I wish to goodness they'd have let Stan out of the Funny Farm just this one night!
FERN. How is Stan?
MAPLE. Just as chipper as a newborn. Claims he's gonna redecorate our house, once he gets a little more confident with his macrame.
CARLA. Isn't that nice.
MAPLE. Yeah, I'm kinda hoping this is just a stage, you know, one of the many steps in the healing process. It'd be a shame if he got stuck here in the macrame stage, couldn't move on.
FERN. When you get to spring him?
MAPLE. Friday.
FERN. Morning? Afternoon?
MAPLE. Oh, I don't know. Some time after milk and cookies and before sedation, I guess.

FERN. They think he's ready to get back to the hustle bustle world of produce?

MAPLE. Tell you the truth, it's kinda hard to tell. He's so sedated, you could stretch him out, take a nap on him.

FERN. That right?

MAPLE. Yeah ... They got some drugs in there, Fern, that would have you whistling Dixie through Woolworth's in no time.

FERN. You don't say.

MAPLE. I didn't mean to imply ... You know I'd never suggest that, Fern ...

(There is an awkward moment between the WOMEN before MAPLE looks down at the baby.)

MAPLE. Oh, will you look at that precious little pumpkin? Will you just look at that pumpkin pie? How's my little waffle today? Are you gonna miss your Maple, cupcake? I'm gonna miss your little muffin face something terrible.

(FERN and CARLA give each other pathetic looks.)

MAPLE. Oh, boo, boo, boo, boo. (*MAPLE has her head in the crib, making the baby smile.*) Oh, boo, boo, boo, boo, boo. There's that little smile. There's that little muffin smile ... (*SHE looks up at Fern and Carla.*) Good Lord, what's the matter with you two?

FERN. Maple, why don't you and Stan go ahead and adopt a baby?
MAPLE. Oh, that's what was making you look so sickly.
CARLA. Yeah Maple, honey, I don't think that's the kind of thing they can cure over at the silly house.
MAPLE. Yeah, but we sure have had fun trying.
FERN. You mean, you two ... ?
MAPLE. Well, he has a private room.
CARLA. What?
FERN. You know.
CARLA. You mean you two did it in the silly house?!
MAPLE. He has a private room.
FERN. Weren't you afraid someone'd walk in on you?
CARLA. Now, I know they don't allow locks in there.
MAPLE. Oh, Stan jammed his head up against the door, so no one could get in.

(Pause.)

FERN. That's kinda hard to picture, Maple.
CARLA. Always said that man had a unique imagination.
MAPLE. Well, he has a private room.

(THEY ALL laugh.)

MAPLE. Wonder what's taking Arnold so long.

CARLA. Must be looking for that special pair of putrid pants.

FERN. Great.

MAPLE. Fern, you're gonna do fine. I'll be with you, and Arnold ...

FERN. Yeah, but how do you lean on a man wears little white cleaty shoes?

MAPLE. Fern.

FERN. Perry Como sweaters.

MAPLE. Fern.

FERN. Still waiting for that sign from Upstairs, I guess.

MAPLE. You're not waiting for a sign, you're waiting for an explosion. Earthquake. For the Man Upstairs to make a personal appearance.

FERN. Could be ...

(The SISTERS look at each other for a moment. CARLA looks out the door.)

CARLA. Say you're waiting for a sign, Fern?

FERN. Guess I am, Carla, yeah ... guess I am.

CARLA. Well, look no further. I believe there's one walking across the street in a pair of tangerine pants.

(THEY all look out the screen door as ARNOLD approaches. ARNOLD enters in a horrendous pair of trousers.)

FERN. God-a-mighty! You've been saving those!

ARNOLD. What do you think?

FERN. I think, if they buried you in those, the ground would spit you back up.

ARNOLD. Thought you'd like 'em ... Now, you, on the other hand, Fern, you just about hang the moon tonight, I tell you what!

FERN. (*Blushes.*) Just an old dress.

ARNOLD. Well, you sure are looking awful uptown, shoot. I tell you what! ... Well, how about that sparkly sky, girls? Carla, you coming with us?

CARLA. Not on your life ... It's the new moon. I haven't been in a car on the day of the new moon in over ...

ARNOLD. Carla.

CARLA. Arnold, you don't understand, I haven't been in a car in ...

ARNOLD. Carla.

CARLA. Ok, ok, sure. Sure I'll go. If you're prepared to drive me over to the silly house when you catch me foaming at the mouth in your rear-view mirror ...

MAPLE. Carla.

CARLA. Back in the back seat, rolled up in the feudal position, sucking on my shoes.

ARNOLD. Carla!

CARLA. (*Looks at Fern. Pause.*) Hate to miss a party.

ARNOLD. That's the spirit.

MAPLE. You want me to pack some kind of a diaper bag, Fern?

FERN. I'm not sure, I ... I've been worried about the baby all day, afraid she might be coming down with something.

ARNOLD. What do you mean, Fern?

FERN. She looks to me like she's turnin' a little green.

MAPLE. Green? (*Looks at the baby.*)

FERN. Yeah, she just doesn't look right to me. Looks a little green. I don't know, I just don't feel right taking her out tonight.

MAPLE. Well, goodness, Fern, I'll stay with her.

ARNOLD. Maple, you shouldn't have to ...

MAPLE. Oh Arnold, I don't care about ...

FERN. No, please, it could be nothing's wrong with her and I'd feel so stupid making one of you stay with her, just 'cause I'm seeing green.

MAPLE. But Fern, that seems so unfair when...

FERN. Please, I ...

ARNOLD. It's just a matter of sitting in the car...

FERN. I know all that, but ...

ARNOLD. The minute you wanna come home...

FERN. I know, but ...

MAPLE. We'll all be there with you.

FERN. I'm aware of all that ... Please.

MAPLE. Oh, Fern ...

FERN. Maple, please!

MAPLE. But that night out at the Super Krogers...
FERN. Forget the Super Krogers!
MAPLE. But ...
FERN. Forget it! Could we just forget that ever happened? Huh?! You don't just ... You don't just flip a switch and the lights come back on! It's gotta come from ... from ... I don't know where it's gotta come from, but not from some dumb raffle! Some stupid stinking raffle! Forget it! Forget it ever happened! FORGET THE SUPER GODDAMNED KROGERS!!!

(Pause as FERN and MAPLE look at each other.)

MAPLE. You got it, Fern.
FERN. I'm sorry.
MAPLE. Nope. That's what you want, Fern, that's what you get. Come on, you two, we'll just catch the finale at this rate.

(MAPLE, holding the baby in one arm, drags CARLA out the door with the other. ARNOLD hesitates. FERN runs to the door.)

FERN. (*To the women, as THEY walk away.*) Please don't walk away looking so sour, I hate that! Tell you what I'll do, I'll turn off all the lights, and light my hair on fire, and jump around screaming OOOO and AAAAH and have me a big old time! What do you think of that, huh?!

I'll have me a wing-ding! You'll wish you'd stayed! ... I'm sorry, Arnold.

ARNOLD. No, I'm the one who should be sorry ... Spent the last four weeks out here on your couch and I'm acting like I spent them inside your head ... What is it you call that again? What you have?

FERN. Agoraphobia.

ARNOLD. Agoraphobia, huh. Awful big word to be carrying around with you for so long ... Ag-or-a-phob-i-a ... Hm. Where did you find that? Magazine?

FERN. Yep.

ARNOLD. Same place Brenda found "Eating Disorder." What do you think of that? Next thing you know we'll be reading about "Bernice's Hair." Yep, that "Bernice's Hair" is bad, you let it get out of hand, apt to wind up in the hospital. I knew a fellow who had that, once. "Bernice's Hair" ... Shooo, yeah, that's a bad one ...

FERN. What are you getting at, Arnold?

ARNOLD. Fellow gets married, wants a baby. Not too much to ask for, just a little baby to love. So he tries a while, prays a little, tries some more, prays harder, tries again, prays with a vengeance, tries one more time and gives up praying. After twelve years all he gets is a big dial tone in the sky. Figures the Man Upstairs must have fallen asleep, changed neighborhoods, got the stereo cranked too high. So he dreams up something to get His attention. Things get a little out of hand, and next thing you know, the police pick him up driving around in his wife's

Oldsmobile, wearing somebody else's hair. Bernice's hair ... Heck, we've all been there, one time or another. You gotta give Stan credit, I believe if I were looking out from on high, and saw a fellow driving around in somebody else's blond bouffant hairdo, I'd stick around long enough to hear him out. That's all any of us really wants, isn't it? ... Isn't it Fern? ... Somebody to stick around long enough to hear us out.

FERN. (*Pause.*) I'm happy in here, Arnold.

ARNOLD. (*Pause.*) I can't swallow that, Fern. Just won't go down.

FERN. Then maybe you've stuck around too long.

(HE watches her for a moment before HE walks out the door. HE lets the screen door slam as he goes, setting off the dog-barking machine.)

FERN. AAAAHHHHHHHHHHHHHHHH! (*SHE runs over and destroys the dog-barking machine. Pointing up to the heavens.*) You sent him over here, didn't you? Well, he's an irritant! ... A GODDAMNED IRRITANT! (*SHE covers her mouth.*) Sorry ... You're welcome to use my name in vain if you'd like. Ferndamned ... He's a Ferndamned irritant, and you can take him back!

(SHE goes around the room turning off the lights. SHE stands in the middle of the room, and suddenly punches the air. SHE kicks her shoes

off across the room. SHE takes her earrings off and throws them across the room. SHE kicks and punches the air some more and finally collapses on the floor. SHE rolls up in a little ball and rocks herself. Finally ARNOLD appears at the door, holding a lit sparkler. HE stands there watching Fern for a moment.)

FERN. That you, Arnold?
ARNOLD. Yep.

(ARNOLD enters, and sits on the couch behind her.
Pause.)

FERN. There was a kid in my neighborhood, had terrible asthma. Walked around with a breathalizer, that kind of thing. One day a bunch of us were swimming out at the Brown County pool. We were trying to see who could hold their breath and swim from one side of the pool to the other, when this kid with the asthma has the empty-headed idea that maybe he'd like to try it, too. So, he jumps in and starts swimming like mad for the other side. Everybody stops what they're doing to watch him. It was like every single one of us was jammed inside that kid's lungs, and we could all feel 'em ripping apart, 'bout to burst. He's kicking and thrashing when finally, he makes it, pulls himself up, turns around, and sees all our beaming faces. When the kid's finally able to suck enough air back in, he bursts into tears. His papa runs over and asks him why it is he's crying, and he points at all of us and says, (*Starts to cry.*) "It's hope, Papa, it's all this hope that's killing me!"

(*SHE buries her head in her hands while ARNOLD looks out and thinks. Pause.*)

ARNOLD. I can see what you're saying, Fern, but I'm afraid it's dug in so deep, we're stuck with it.
FERN. I believe you're right, Arnold ... Hope has reared it's ugly head.

(*Pause.*)

ARNOLD. (*Gets up and holds his hand out to her.*) Can you go any further, Fern?
FERN. (*Looks at him.*) Yes, Arnold, I believe I can go further.

(*SHE takes his hand and HE leads her to the door, where SHE hesitates.*)

ARNOLD. Any further?

(*Pause.*)

FERN. Yes.

(HE holds the door for her as SHE steps out onto the front stoop. ARNOLD steps out after her. FERN looks up at the night sky, and we hear the SOUNDS of a southern summer night, e.g., cicadas and crickets.)

FERN. Arnold?
ARNOLD. What's that, Fern?
FERN. What is your name, anyhow?

(HE puts his arm around her, as the LIGHTS fade.)

THE END

COSTUME PLOT

FERN: T-shirt, shorts, sneakers, sun dress, sandals

ARNOLD: golf shirts (3), plaid pants, Perry Como sweater, white shoes, plaid shorts, tangerine pants, plaid jacket

MAPLE: jumper, shirt to go under jumper, sun dress, tennis shoes, pair of pumps

CARLA: long shirts with large shoulder pads (3), stretch slacks (3), high heels (3 pair), jacket

PROPERTY PLOT

Binoculars
Phone
T V
Couch
Remote control
Knife
Plate of cookies
Magazines
Bag of wigs
Six wigs
Driver's license
Fake baby
Curling iron
Can of Coke
Microwave box
Bottle of whisky
Three glasses
Golf bag with putter
Pillow and blanket
Dog barking machine

(Clutter the set with tons of baby paraphernalia. Stuffed animals, diaper boxes, mobiles, wet wipes, etc.)

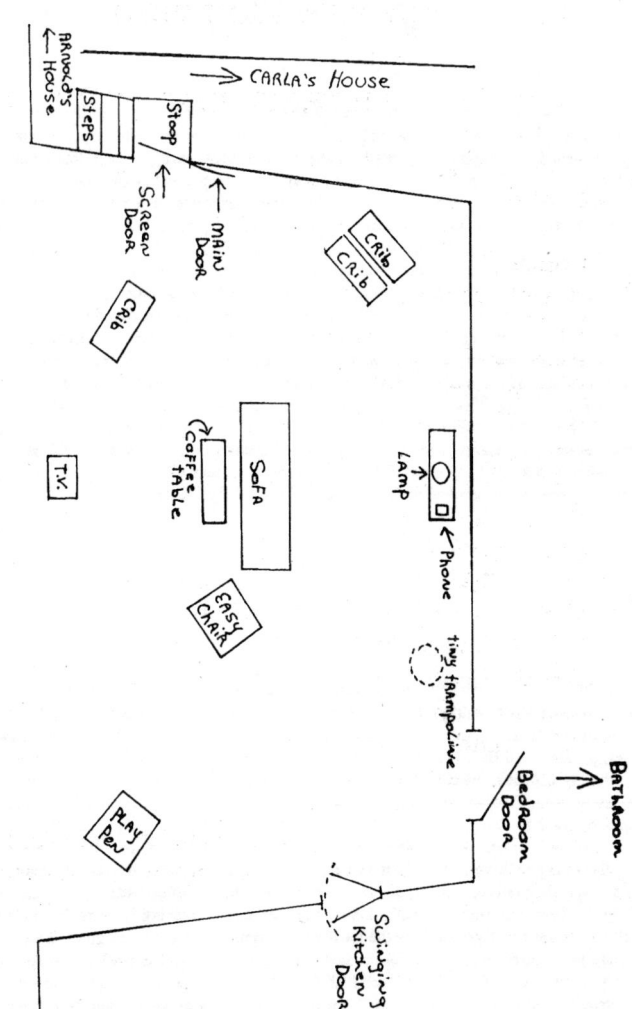

THE BABY DANCE
Little Theatre-Drama
by Jane Anderson

3m., 2f. 2 Ints. Stephanie Zimbalist starred in the original production of this brilliant, moving new drama, both at the Pasadena Playhouse and at the Long Wharf Theatre. She played a woman from Los Angeles named Rachel who has everything she wants in life—except a child. Rachel has located a poor couple who have more children than they can afford to keep, and have agreed to let their latest, when it is born, be adopted by Rachel and her husband. Desperate for a healthy baby, Rachel is paying for all of the poor woman's pre-natal care and hospital expenses. When she arrives for a visit at the trailer park where Al and Wanda live, she is appalled to find that Wanda is not eating correctly. She is also appalled by Al, who actually comes on to her when he is not seething with resentment. The whole arrangement nearly falls through, but by the second act, both couples are back on track. Until, that is, it is learned that the newborn baby may—just may—have suffered some brain damage in the difficult birth, causing Wanda's husband to back away from the deal, much to Rachel's chagrin. Rachel wants the baby anyway, wants to take the chance. In the end, the childless couple do renege on the deal, leaving Wanda and Al with yet another mouth to feed. "The best play produced this season at the Long Wharf Theatre and the first in several seasons to touch the heart so profoundly."—New Haven Advocate. *"The Baby Dance* is not just a 'woman's play.' It is a gripping drama that leaves the audience with more empathy for these people than they would have thought possible."—Bridgeport Post. "A powerful, deeply wrenching drama."—Berkshire Eagle. "It would take a heart of stone to be unmoved by Jane Anderson's *The Baby Dance*.". (#4305)

THE BATTLE OF SHALLOWFORD
Little Theatre-Comedy
by Ed Simpson

8m., 1f. Int. On a quiet Sunday night, the local regulars have gathered at Burton Mock's general store, in the small town of Shallowford, NC. It is October, 1938. The rest of the world is poised on the brink of war, but the locals aren't much worried about events in the world at large. They're more interested in the local gossip—and Burton's general store is the best place to hear it. The regulars include the gossipy, whining Clunette; fey church choirmaster Fred; lowlife, wild-eyed Newsome Jarvis, on hand with his "slow" son, Doodad; Mr. Roy, a one-armed World War I veteran who holds court at the store; egotistic local football hero Dewey Sowers; Burton's restless young daughter, Ruthie; and her schoolmate Lonny Hutchins, a sci-fi aficionado. All is calm; until, that is, they turn on the radio and learn that the Martians have invaded! Of course, it is the famous Orson Welles broadcast they are listening to—but they fall for it hook, line and shotgun, and run out to do battle against the fearsome threat from the invading Martians. Only Lonny suspects that something is fishy, but he's got his hands full if he thinks he's gonna deter the local yokels from their moment of glory. This delightful new comedy has had several successful productions nation-wide, and is finally available to y'all. Read it if you want a good laugh; produce it if that's how you like your audience to respond. "A theatrical gem."—Asheville Citizen-Times. "Tickle their funny bones, warm their hearts, don't insult their intelligence … Ed Simpson's *The Battle of Shallowford* hits that magic trio."—Knoxville News-Sentinel. "A sentimental comedy that's hilariously on target. It could easily become a community theatre staple in much the way the works of Larry Shue have."—Knoxville Journal. A cassette tape of excerpts from the Mercury Theatre's radio broadcast of "The War of the Worlds" called for in the text of the play is available for $10, plus postage. (#4315)